MORNING IN THE BURNED HOUSE

BOOKS BY MARGARET ATWOOD

FICTION
The Edible Woman
Surfacing
Lady Oracle
Life Before Man
Bodily Harm
The Handmaid's Tale
Cat's Eye
The Robber Bride

SHORT FICTION
Dancing Girls
Bluebeard's Egg
Murder in the Dark
Wilderness Tips
Good Bones

POETRY
The Circle Game
The Animals in That Country
The Journals of Susanna Moodie
Procedures for Underground
Power Politics
You Are Happy
Two-Headed Poems
True Stories
Interlunar
Selected Poems
Selected Poems II
Morning in the Burned House

NON-FICTION
Survival: A Thematic Guide to Canadian Literature
Second Words

MARGARET ATWOOD

MORNING
IN THE
BURNED
HOUSE

HOUGHTON MIFFLIN COMPANY

BOSTON   NEW YORK

For information about permission to reproduce selections from this
book, write to trade.permissions@hmhco.com or to
Permissions, Houghton Mifflin Harcourt Publishing Company,
3 Park Avenue, 19th Floor, New York, New York 10016.

www.hmhco.com

Library of Congress Cataloging-in-Publication Data
Atwood, Margaret Eleanor, date.
Morning in the burned house / Margaret Atwood.
p.   cm.
ISBN 0-395-75591-3
ISBN 0-395-82521-0 (pbk.)
ISBN 978-0-395-82521-1
I. Title.
PR9199.3.A8M67   1995B
811'.54 — dc20   95-22797
CIP

First published in Canada in 1995 by
McClelland & Stewart Inc.

Printed in the United States of America
DOH 24 23 22 21 20 19 18 17 16
4500636643

For my family

ACKNOWLEDGMENTS

Some of these poems have appeared in: *The Atlantic Monthly, Carnage Hall Magazine, Field, Harper's, Islands of Hope* (Firefly Books), *The Michigan Quarterly Review, Mississippi Valley Review, New Letters, The North American Review, The Paris Review, Ploughshares, River Styx, This Magazine, The Times Literary Supplement,* and *vice Versa.*

CONTENTS

I.

You Come Back   3
A Sad Child   4
In the Secular Night   6
Waiting   8
February   11
Asparagus   13
Red Fox   16

II.

Miss July Grows Older   21
Manet's Olympia   24
Daphne and Laura and So Forth   26
Cressida to Troilus: A Gift   28
Ava Gardner Reincarnated as a Magnolia   30
Helen of Troy Does Counter Dancing   33
A Man Looks   37
Sekhmet, The Lion-Headed Goddess of War,
    Violent Storms, Pestilence, and Recovery
    From Illness, Contemplates the Desert
    in The Metropolitan Museum of Art   39

III.

Romantic   45
Cell   47
The Loneliness of the Military Historian   49
Marsh Languages   54
Frogless   56
Half-hanged Mary   58
Owl Burning   70
Down   72
A Pink Hotel in California   76

IV.

Man in a Glacier   81
Wave   83
King Lear in Respite Care   85
A Visit   88
Dancing   90
Bored   91
Flowers   93
Two Dreams   96
The Time   98
Two Dreams, 2   99
Oh   101
The Ottawa River by Night   103

v.

Vermilion Flycatcher,
     San Pedro River, Arizona   107
The Moment   109
Up   110
Girl Without Hands   112
The Signer   114
A Fire Place   116
Statuary   118
Shapechangers in Winter   120
Morning in the Burned House   126

MORNING IN THE BURNED HOUSE

I

YOU COME BACK

You come back into the room
where you've been living
all along. You say:
What's been going on
while I was away? Who
got those sheets dirty, and why
are there no more grapefruit?
Setting foot on the middle ground
between body and word, which contains,
or is supposed to, other
people. You know it was you
who slept, who ate here, though you don't
believe it. I must have taken
time off, you think, for the buttered
toast and the love and maybe both
at once, which would account for the
grease on the bedspread, but no,
now you're certain, someone else
has been here wearing
your clothes and saying
words for you, because there was no time off.

You're sad because you're sad.
It's psychic. It's the age. It's chemical.
Go see a shrink or take a pill,
or hug your sadness like an eyeless doll
you need to sleep.

Well, all children are sad
but some get over it.
Count your blessings. Better than that,
buy a hat. Buy a coat or pet.
Take up dancing to forget.

Forget what?
Your sadness, your shadow,
whatever it was that was done to you
the day of the lawn party
when you came inside flushed with the sun,
your mouth sulky with sugar,
in your new dress with the ribbon
and the ice-cream smear,
and said to yourself in the bathroom,
I am not the favourite child.

4

My darling, when it comes
right down to it
and the light fails and the fog rolls in
and you're trapped in your overturned body
under a blanket or burning car,

and the red flame is seeping out of you
and igniting the tarmac beside your head
or else the floor, or else the pillow,
none of us is;
or else we all are.

IN THE SECULAR NIGHT

In the secular night you wander around
alone in your house. It's two-thirty.
Everyone has deserted you,
or this is your story;
you remember it from being sixteen,
when the others were out somewhere, having a good
    time,
or so you suspected,
and you had to baby-sit.
You took a large scoop of vanilla ice-cream
and filled up the glass with grapejuice
and ginger ale, and put on Glenn Miller
with his big-band sound,
and lit a cigarette and blew the smoke up the chimney,
and cried for a while because you were not dancing,
and then danced, by yourself, your mouth circled with
    purple.

Now, forty years later, things have changed,
and it's baby lima beans.
It's necessary to reserve a secret vice.
This is what comes from forgetting to eat
at the stated mealtimes. You simmer them carefully,

drain, add cream and pepper,
and amble up and down the stairs,
scooping them up with your fingers right out of the
    bowl,
talking to yourself out loud.
You'd be surprised if you got an answer,
but that part will come later.

There is so much silence between the words,
you say. You say, The sensed absence
of God and the sensed presence
amount to much the same thing,
only in reverse.
You say, I have too much white clothing.
You start to hum.
Several hundred years ago
this could have been mysticism
or heresy. It isn't now.
Outside there are sirens.
Someone's been run over.
The century grinds on.

WAITING

Here it is then, the dark thing,
the dark thing you have waited for so long.
You have made such melodramas.

You thought it would carry its own mist,
obscuring you in a damp enfolding, like the mildew
shroud on bread. Or you thought it would hide
in your closet, among the clothes you outgrew years ago,
nesting in dustballs and fallen hair, shedding
one of your fabricated skins
after another and growing bigger,
honing its teeth on your discarded
cloth lives, and then it would pounce
from the inside out, and your heart
would be filled with roaring

or else that it would come swiftly and without sound,
but with one pitiless glaring eye, like a high-speed train,
and a single blow on the head and then blackout.

Instead it is strangely like home.
Like your own home, fifty years ago,
in December, in the early evening

when the indoor light changed, from clear to clouded,
a clouded thick yellow, like a sulphury eggyolk,

and the reading lamp was turned on
with its brown silk shade, its aroma
of hot copper, the living
room flickering in the smells of cooking dinner,

and you crouched on the hardwood floor, smudged
    elbows
and scaly winter knees on the funny papers,
listening to the radio, news of disasters
that made you feel safe,
like the voice of your mother
urging you yet again to set the table
you are doing your best to ignore,
and you realized for the first time
in your life that you would be old

some day, you would some day be
as old as you are now,
and the home you were reading the funnies in
by the thick yellow light, would be gone
with all the people in it, even you,
even you in your young, smudgy body
with its scent of newsprint and dirty

knees and washed cotton,
and you would have a different body
by then, an old murky one,
a stranger's body you could not even imagine,
and you would be lost and alone.

And now it is now
and the dark thing is here,
and after all it is nothing new;
it is only a memory, after all:
a memory of a fear,
a yellowing paper child's fear
you have long since forgotten
and that has now come true.

Winter. Time to eat fat
and watch hockey. In the pewter mornings, the cat,
a black fur sausage with yellow
Houdini eyes, jumps up on the bed and tries
to get onto my head. It's his
way of telling whether or not I'm dead.
If I'm not, he wants to be scratched; if I am
he'll think of something. He settles
on my chest, breathing his breath
of burped-up meat and musty sofas,
purring like a washboard. Some other tomcat,
not yet a capon, has been spraying our front door,
declaring war. It's all about sex and territory,
which are what will finish us off
in the long run. Some cat owners around here
should snip a few testicles. If we wise
hominids were sensible, we'd do that too,
or eat our young, like sharks.
But it's love that does us in. Over and over
again, *He shoots, he scores!* and famine
crouches in the bedsheets, ambushing the pulsing
eiderdown, and the windchill factor hits
thirty below, and pollution pours

out of our chimneys to keep us warm.
February, month of despair,
with a skewered heart in the centre.
I think dire thoughts, and lust for French fries
with a splash of vinegar.
Cat, enough of your greedy whining
and your small pink bumhole.
Off my face! You're the life principle,
more or less, so get going
on a little optimism around here.
Get rid of death. Celebrate increase. Make it be spring.

ASPARAGUS

This afternoon a man leans over
the hard rolls and the curled
butter, and tells me everything: two
women love him, he loves them, what
should he do?

        The sun
sifts down through the imperceptibly
brownish urban air. I'm going to
suffer for this: turn red, get
blisters or else cancer. I eat
asparagus with my fingers, he
plunges into description.
He's at his wit's end, sewed
up in his own frenzy. He has
breadcrumbs in his beard.
        I wonder
if I should let my hair go grey
so my advice will be better.
I could wrinkle up my eyelids,
look wise. I could get a pet lizard.
You're not crazy, I tell him.
Others have done this. Me too.

Messy love is better than none,
I guess. I'm no authority
on sane living.

Which is all true
and no help at all, because
this form of love is like the pain
of childbirth: so intense
it's hard to remember afterwards,
or what kind of screams and grimaces
it pushed you into.

The shrimp arrive on their skewers,
the courtyard trees unroll
their yellowy caterpillars,
pollen powders our shoulders.
He wants them both, he relates
tortures, the coffee
arrives, and altogether I am amazed
at his stupidities.

I sit looking at him
with a sort of wonder,
or is it envy?

Listen, I say to him,
you're very lucky.

RED FOX

The red fox crosses the ice
intent on none of my business.
It's winter and slim pickings.

I stand in the bushy cemetery,
pretending to watch birds,
but really watching the fox
who could care less.
She pauses on the sheer glare
of the pond. She knows I'm there,
sniffs me in the wind at her shoulder.
If I had a gun or dog
or a raw heart, she'd smell it.
She didn't get this smart for nothing.

She's a lean vixen: I can see
the ribs, the sly
trickster's eyes, filled with longing
and desperation, the skinny
feet, adept at lies.

Why encourage the notion
of virtuous poverty?

It's only an excuse
for zero charity.
Hunger corrupts, and absolute hunger
corrupts absolutely,
or almost. Of course there are mothers,
squeezing their breasts
dry, pawning their bodies,
shedding teeth for their children,
or that's our fond belief.
But remember – Hansel
and Gretel were dumped in the forest
because their parents were starving.
Sauve qui peut. To survive
we'd all turn thief

and rascal, or so says the fox,
with her coat of an elegant scoundrel,
her white knife of a smile,
who knows just where she's going:

to steal something
that doesn't belong to her –
some chicken, or one more chance,
or other life.

II

II

How much longer can I get away
with being so fucking cute?
Not much longer.
The shoes with bows, the cunning underwear
with slogans on the crotch – *Knock Here*,
and so forth –
will have to go, along with the cat suit.
After a while you forget
what you really look like.
You think your mouth is the size it was.
You pretend not to care.

When I was young I went with my hair
hiding one eye, thinking myself daring;
off to the movies in my jaunty pencil
skirt and elastic cinch-belt,
chewed gum, left lipstick
imprints the shape of grateful, rubbery
sighs on the cigarettes of men
I hardly knew and didn't want to.
Men were a skill, you had to have
good hands, breathe into

their nostrils, as for horses. It was something I did well,
like playing the flute, although I don't.

In the forests of grey stems there are standing pools,
tarn-coloured, choked with brown leaves.
Through them you can see an arm, a shoulder,
when the light is right, with the sky clouded.
The train goes past silos, through meadows,
the winter wheat on the fields like scanty fur.

I still get letters, although not many.
A man writes me, requesting true-life stories
about bad sex. He's doing an anthology.
He got my name off an old calendar,
the photo that's mostly bum and daisies,
back when my skin had the golden slick
of fresh-spread margarine.
Not rape, he says, but disappointment,
more like a defeat of expectations.
Dear Sir, I reply, I never had any.
Bad sex, that is.
It was never the sex, it was the other things,
the absence of flowers, the death threats,
the eating habits at breakfast.
I notice I'm using the past tense.

Though the vaporous cloud of chemicals that enveloped
    you
like a glowing eggshell, an incense,
doesn't disappear: it just gets larger
and takes in more. You grow out
of sex like a shrunk dress
into your common senses, those you share
with whatever's listening. The way the sun
moves through the hours becomes important,
the smeared raindrops
on the window, buds
on the roadside weeds, the sheen
of spilled oil on a raw ditch
filling with muddy water.

Don't get me wrong: with the lights out
I'd still take on anyone,
if I had the energy to spare.
But after a while these flesh arpeggios get boring,
like Bach over and over;
too much of one kind of glory.

When I was all body I was lazy.
I had an easy life, and was not grateful.
Now there are more of me.
Don't confuse me with my hen-leg elbows:
what you get is no longer
what you see.

MANET'S OLYMPIA

She reclines, more or less.
Try that posture, it's hardly languor.
Her right arm sharp angles.
With her left she conceals her ambush.
Shoes but not stockings,
how sinister. The flower
behind her ear is naturally
not real, of a piece
with the sofa's drapery.
The windows (if any) are shut.
This is indoor sin.
Above the head of the (clothed) maid
is an invisible voice balloon: *Slut.*

But. Consider the body,
unfragile, defiant, the pale nipples
staring you right in the bull's-eye.
Consider also the black ribbon
around the neck. What's under it?
A fine red threadline, where the head
was taken off and glued back on.
The body's on offer,
         neck's as far as it goes.

4

This is no morsel.
Put clothes on her and you'd have a schoolteacher,
the kind with the brittle whiphand.

There's someone else in this room.
You, Monsieur Voyeur.
As for that object of yours
she's seen those before, and better.

I, the head, am the only subject
of this picture.
You, Sir, are furniture.
Get stuffed.

DAPHNE AND LAURA AND SO FORTH

He was the one who saw me
just before I changed,
before bark/fur/snow closed over
my mouth, before my eyes grew eyes.

I should not have shown fear,
or so much leg.

His look of disbelief —
I didn't mean to!
Just, her neck was so much more
fragile than I thought.

The gods don't listen to reason,
they need what they need —
that suntan line at the bottom
of the spine, those teeth like mouthwash,
that drop of sweat pearling
the upper lip —
or that's what gets said in court.

Why talk when you can whisper?
Rustle, like dried leaves.
Under the bed.

It's ugly here, but safer.
I have eight fingers
and a shell, and live in corners.
I'm free to stay up all night.
I'm working on
these ideas of my own:
venom, a web, a hat,
some last resort.

He was running,
he was asking something,
he wanted something or other.

You forced me to give you poisonous gifts.
I can put this no other way.
Everything I gave was to get rid of you
as one gives to a beggar: *There. Go away.*
The first time, the first sentence even
was in answer to your silent clamour
and not for love, and therefore not
a gift, but to get you out of my hair
or whatever part of me you had slid into
by stealth, by creeping up the stairs,

so that whenever I turned, watering
the narcissus, brushing my teeth,
there you were, just barely, in the corner
of my eye. Peripheral. A floater. No one
ever told you greed and hunger
are not the same.

How did all of this start?
With Pity, that flimsy angel,
with her wet pink eyes and slippery wings
of mucous membrane.
She causes so much trouble.

But nothing I ever gave was good for you;
it was like white bread to goldfish.
They cram and cram, and it kills them,
and they drift in the pool, belly-up,
making stunned faces
and playing on our guilt
as if their own toxic gluttony
was not their fault.

There you are still, outside the window,
still with your hands out, still
pallid and fishy-eyed, still acting
stupidly innocent and starved.

Well, take this then. Have some more body.
Drink and eat.
You'll just make yourself sick. Sicker.
You won't be cured.

Somehow I never succeeded
in being taken seriously. They made me
wear things that were ruffled: off-the-
shoulder blouses, the tiered skirts
of flouncing Spanish dancers, though I never
quite got the hauteur — I was always tempted
to wink, show instead of a tragic
outstretched neck, a slice of flank. Now look
at me: a vaginal hot pink,
vibrant as a laxative bottle —
not, given the company, a respectable
colour. Let's face it: when I was in
the flesh, to be beautiful and to be
a woman was a kind
of joke. The men wanted to nail
me in the trophy room, on the pool-
table if possible, the women simply to poke
my eyes out. Me, I would have preferred
to enjoy myself — a little careless
love, some laughs, a few drinks —
but that was not an option.

What would have given
me weight? Substance? For them.
Long canines? Vengeance?
A stiletto hidden in my skirt,
a greyish rainbow of fate
like an aureole of rancid lard —
or better: dress up in armour,
ride across the steppes, leading a horde
of armed murderers. That gets you a statue,
copper or stone, with a lofty frown
— jaw clenched as if chewing —
like those erected by the sober
citizens, years later,
for all the sad destroyers.

Well, to hell with them. I'd rather
be a flower, even this one, so much like
a toilet-paper decoration
at a high-school dance.
Even that, to be trampled
underfoot next day by the janitor
sweeping up, even the damp flirtation,
the crumpled tulle, even the botched smooch
in the parking lot, the boy with the fat neck
and the hip flask, even the awkward fumbling
with the wired bodice, cheap perfume between

the freckled breasts, would have been better
than all their history, the smudged
flags, dry parchments, layers of dead bone
they find so solemn, the slaughters
they like to memorize, and tell
their children also to pray to

here, where they hate bouquets, the pleasures
of thoughtless botany, a glass
of wine or two on the terrace,
bare leg against white trouser
under the table, that ancient ploy
and vital puzzle, water-
of-life cliché that keeps things going,
tawdry and priceless, the breeze
that riffles through what now
may be my leaves, my green closed
eyes, my negligible
vulgar fragile incandescent petals,
these many mouths, lipsticked and showy
and humid as kisses opening
in a hothouse, oh I'd give anything
to have it back again, in
the flesh, the flesh,
which was all the time
I ever had for anything. The joy.

32

The world is full of women
who'd tell me I should be ashamed of myself
if they had the chance. Quit dancing.
Get some self-respect
and a day job.
Right. And minimum wage,
and varicose veins, just standing
in one place for eight hours
behind a glass counter
bundled up to the neck, instead of
naked as a meat sandwich.
Selling gloves, or something.
Instead of what I do sell.
You have to have talent
to peddle a thing so nebulous
and without material form.
Exploited, they'd say. Yes, any way
you cut it, but I've a choice
of how, and I'll take the money.

I do give value.
Like preachers, I sell vision,
like perfume ads, desire

33

or its facsimile. Like jokes
or war, it's all in the timing.
I sell men back their worst suspicions:
that everything's for sale,
and piecemeal. They gaze at me and see
a chain-saw murder just before it happens,
when thigh, ass, inkblot, crevice, tit, and nipple
are still connected.
Such hatred leaps in them,
my beery worshippers! That, or a bleary
hopeless love. Seeing the rows of heads
and upturned eyes, imploring
but ready to snap at my ankles,
I understand floods and earthquakes, and the urge
to step on ants. I keep the beat,
and dance for them because
they can't. The music smells like foxes,
crisp as heated metal
searing the nostrils
or humid as August, hazy and languorous
as a looted city the day after,
when all the rape's been done
already, and the killing,
and the survivors wander around
looking for garbage
to eat, and there's only a bleak exhaustion.

34

Speaking of which, it's the smiling
tires me out the most.
This, and the pretence
that I can't hear them.
And I can't, because I'm after all
a foreigner to them.
The speech here is all warty gutturals,
obvious as a slab of ham,
but I come from the province of the gods
where meanings are lilting and oblique.
I don't let on to everyone,
but lean close, and I'll whisper:
My mother was raped by a holy swan.
You believe that? You can take me out to dinner.
That's what we tell all the husbands.
There sure are a lot of dangerous birds around.

Not that anyone here
but you would understand.
The rest of them would like to watch me
and feel nothing. Reduce me to components
as in a clock factory or abattoir.
Crush out the mystery.
Wall me up alive
in my own body.
They'd like to see through me,

but nothing is more opaque
than absolute transparency.
Look – my feet don't hit the marble!
Like breath or a balloon, I'm rising,
I hover six inches in the air
in my blazing swan-egg of light.
You think I'm not a goddess?
Try me.
This is a torch song.
Touch me and you'll burn.

A man looks at a beautiful woman
who is trying to get him through a door,
him and his leg-brace: clumsy hammered
carapace of metal,
shrapnel on the outside of his body
from a war he must have forgotten
or never fought. Some spike
on him is caught down there. She bends over
and he looks at her graceful rump, and thinks *rump*,
and then thinks: *pear on a plate*,
and, on the underside, two apples.
He can't believe he can be so trite,
like some shoddy derivative painter,
and so removed from her. Aren't those thighs?
Isn't that hair? He opens the thighs, strokes the hair,
nothing stirs. He thinks harder, tries *vulva*;
a word like a part in a car motor,
something made of rubber, an oily valve
that squeezes and turns itself inside out.
No hope for it. Once
he would have been able to smell her,
pungency of spring pond and soft onions
mixed with a coy deodorant,

eyelet and armpit, and beyond that
the murmur of willows, leaves
of sunlit weeds crushed under her,
but now she has no such halo.

She stands up and smiles at him,
a smile so translucent
he wrinkles in it, like the skin
on steamed milk.
He's nothing to her but luggage
she needs to haul from room to room,
or a sick dog to be kind to.
She says, "Shall we try again?"
He thinks, *I am angry.* She takes his arm.
He thinks, *I will die soon.*

SEKHMET, THE LION-HEADED GODDESS OF WAR, VIOLENT STORMS, PESTILENCE, AND RECOVERY FROM ILLNESS, CONTEMPLATES THE DESERT IN THE METROPOLITAN MUSEUM OF ART

He was the sort of man
who wouldn't hurt a fly.
Many flies are now alive
while he is not.
He was not my patron.
He preferred full granaries, I battle.
My roar meant slaughter.
Yet here we are together
in the same museum.
That's not what I see, though, the fitful
crowds of staring children
learning the lesson of multi-
cultural obliteration, *sic transit*
and so on.

I see the temple where I was born
or built, where I held power.
I see the desert beyond,
where the hot conical tombs, that look
from a distance, frankly, like dunces' hats,

hide my jokes: the dried-out flesh
and bones, the wooden boats
in which the dead sail endlessly
in no direction.

What did you expect from gods
with animal heads?
Though come to think of it
the ones made later, who were fully human,
were not such good news either.
Favour me and give me riches,
destroy my enemies.
That seems to be the gist.
Oh yes: *And save me from death.*
In return we're given blood
and bread, flowers and prayer,
and lip service.

Maybe there's something in all of this
I missed. But if it's selfless
love you're looking for,
you've got the wrong goddess.

I just sit where I'm put, composed
of stone and wishful thinking:
that the deity who kills for pleasure

will also heal,
that in the midst of your nightmare,
the final one, a kind lion
will come with bandages in her mouth
and the soft body of a woman,
and lick you clean of fever,
and pick your soul up gently by the nape of the neck
and caress you into darkness and paradise.

III

III

ROMANTIC

Men and their mournful romanticisms
that can't get the dishes done —
that's freedom, that broken wineglass
in the cold fireplace.

When women wash underpants, it's a chore.
When men do it, an intriguing affliction.
How plangent, the damp socks flapping on the line,
how lost and single in the orphaning air . . .

She cherishes that sadness,
tells him to lie down on the grass,
closes each of his eyes with a finger,
applies her body like a poultice.

You poor thing, said the Australian woman
while he held our baby —
as if I had forced him to do it,
as if I had my high heel in his face.

Still, who's taken in?
Every time?
Us, and our empty hands, the hands
of starving nurses.

It's bullet holes we want to see in their skin,
scars, and the chance to touch them.

Now look objectively. You have to
admit the cancer cell is beautiful.
If it were a flower, you'd say, *How pretty*,
with its mauve centre and pink petals

or if a cover for a pulpy thirties
sci-fi magazine, *How striking*;
as an alien, a success,
all purple eye and jelly tentacles
and spines, or are they gills,
creeping around on granular Martian
dirt red as the inside of the body,

while its tender walls
expand and burst, its spores
scatter elsewhere, take root, like money,
drifting like a fiction or
miasma in and out of people's
brains, digging themselves
industriously in. The lab technician

says, *It has forgotten
how to die*. But why remember? All it wants is more

amnesia. More life, and more abundantly. To take
more. To eat more. To replicate itself. To keep on
doing those things forever. Such desires
are not unknown. Look in the mirror.

Confess: it's my profession
that alarms you.
This is why few people ask me to dinner,
though Lord knows I don't go out of my way to be scary.
I wear dresses of sensible cut
and unalarming shades of beige,
I smell of lavender and go to the hairdresser's:
no prophetess mane of mine,
complete with snakes, will frighten the youngsters.
If I roll my eyes and mutter,
if I clutch at my heart and scream in horror
like a third-rate actress chewing up a mad scene,
I do it in private and nobody sees
but the bathroom mirror.

In general I might agree with you:
women should not contemplate war,
should not weigh tactics impartially,
or evade the word *enemy*,
or view both sides and denounce nothing.
Women should march for peace,
or hand out white feathers to arouse bravery,

spit themselves on bayonets
to protect their babies,
whose skulls will be split anyway,
or, having been raped repeatedly,
hang themselves with their own hair.
These are the functions that inspire general comfort.
That, and the knitting of socks for the troops
and a sort of moral cheerleading.
Also: mourning the dead.
Sons, lovers, and so forth.
All the killed children.

Instead of this, I tell
what I hope will pass as truth.
A blunt thing, not lovely.
The truth is seldom welcome,
especially at dinner,
though I am good at what I do.
My trade is courage and atrocities.
I look at them and do not condemn.
I write things down the way they happened,
as near as can be remembered.
I don't ask *why*, because it is mostly the same.
Wars happen because the ones who start them
think they can win.

In my dreams there is glamour.
The Vikings leave their fields
each year for a few months of killing and plunder,
much as the boys go hunting.
In real life they were farmers.
They come back loaded with splendour.
The Arabs ride against Crusaders
with scimitars that could sever
silk in the air.
A swift cut to the horse's neck
and a hunk of armour crashes down
like a tower. Fire against metal.
A poet might say: romance against banality.
When awake, I know better.

Despite the propaganda, there are no monsters,
or none that can be finally buried.
Finish one off, and circumstances
and the radio create another.
Believe me: whole armies have prayed fervently
to God all night and meant it,
and been slaughtered anyway.
Brutality wins frequently,
and large outcomes have turned on the invention
of a mechanical device, viz. radar.
True, valour sometimes counts for something,

as at Thermopylae. Sometimes being right –
though ultimate virtue, by agreed tradition,
is decided by the winner.
Sometimes men throw themselves on grenades
and burst like paper bags of guts
to save their comrades.
I can admire that.
But rats and cholera have won many wars.
Those, and potatoes,
or the absence of them.
It's no use pinning all those medals
across the chests of the dead.
Impressive, but I know too much.
Grand exploits merely depress me.

In the interests of research
I have walked on many battlefields
that once were liquid with pulped
men's bodies and spangled with exploded
shells and splayed bone.
All of them have been green again
by the time I got there.
Each has inspired a few good quotes in its day.
Sad marble angels brood like hens
over the grassy nests where nothing hatches.
(The angels could just as well be described as *vulgar*

or *pitiless*, depending on camera angle.)
The word *glory* figures a lot on gateways.
Of course I pick a flower or two
from each, and press it in the hotel Bible
for a souvenir.
I'm just as human as you.

But it's no use asking me for a final statement.
As I say, I deal in tactics.
Also statistics:
for every year of peace there have been four hundred
years of war.

MARSH LANGUAGES

The dark soft languages are being silenced:
Mothertongue Mothertongue Mothertongue
falling one by one back into the moon.

Language of marshes,
language of the roots of rushes tangled
together in the ooze,
marrow cells twinning themselves
inside the warm core of the bone:
pathways of hidden light in the body fade and wink out.

The sibilants and gutturals,
the cave language, the half-light
forming at the back of the throat,
the mouth's damp velvet moulding
the lost syllable for "I" that did not mean separate,
all are becoming sounds no longer
heard because no longer spoken,
and everything that could once be said in them has
    ceased to exist.

The languages of the dying suns
are themselves dying,

but even the word for this has been forgotten.
The mouth against skin, vivid and fading,
can no longer speak both cherishing and farewell.
It is now only a mouth, only skin.
There is no more longing.

Translation was never possible.
Instead there was always only
conquest, the influx
of the language of hard nouns,
the language of metal,
the language of either/or,
the one language that has eaten all the others.

The sore trees cast their leaves
too early. Each twig pinching
shut like a jabbed clam.
Soon there will be a hot gauze of snow
searing the roots.

Booze in the spring runoff,
pure antifreeze;
the stream worms drunk and burning.
Tadpoles wrecked in the puddles.

Here comes an eel with a dead eye
grown from its cheek.
Would you cook it?
You would if.

The people eat sick fish
because there are no others.
Then they get born wrong.

This is not sport, sir.
This is not good weather.
This is not blue and green.

This is home.
Travel anywhere in a year, five years,
and you'll end up here.

HALF-HANGED MARY

("Half-hanged Mary" was Mary Webster, who was accused of witch-craft in the 1680s in a Puritan town in Massachusetts and hanged from a tree — where, according to one of the several surviving accounts, she was left all night. It is known that when she was cut down she was still alive, since she lived for another fourteen years.)

7 p.m.

Rumour was loose in the air,
hunting for some neck to land on.
I was milking the cow,
the barn door open to the sunset.

I didn't feel the aimed word hit
and go in like a soft bullet.
I didn't feel the smashed flesh
closing over it like water
over a thrown stone.

I was hanged for living alone,
for having blue eyes and a sunburned skin,
tattered skirts, few buttons,

a weedy farm in my own name,
and a surefire cure for warts;

Oh yes, and breasts,
and a sweet pear hidden in my body.
Whenever there's talk of demons
these come in handy.

8 p.m.

The rope was an improvisation.
With time they'd have thought of axes.

Up I go like a windfall in reverse,
a blackened apple stuck back onto the tree.

Trussed hands, rag in my mouth,
a flag raised to salute the moon,

old bone-faced goddess, old original,
who once took blood in return for food.

The men of the town stalk homeward,
excited by their show of hate,

their own evil turned inside out like a glove,
and me wearing it.

9 p.m.

The bonnets come to stare,
the dark skirts also,
the upturned faces in between,
mouths closed so tight they're lipless.
I can see down into their eyeholes
and nostrils. I can see their fear.

You were my friend, you too.
I cured your baby, Mrs.,
and flushed yours out of you,
Non-wife, to save your life.

Help me down? You don't dare.
I might rub off on you,
like soot or gossip. Birds
of a feather burn together,
though as a rule ravens are singular.

In a gathering like this one
the safe place is the background,

pretending you can't dance,
the safe stance pointing a finger.

I understand. You can't spare
anything, a hand, a piece of bread, a shawl
against the cold,
a good word. Lord
knows there isn't much
to go around. You need it all.

10 p.m.

Well God, now that I'm up here
with maybe some time to kill
away from the daily
fingerwork, legwork, work
at the hen level,
we can continue our quarrel,
the one about free will.

Is it my choice that I'm dangling
like a turkey's wattles from this
more than indifferent tree?
If Nature is Your alphabet,
what letter is this rope?

Does my twisting body spell out Grace?
I hurt, therefore I am.
Faith, Charity, and Hope
are three dead angels
falling like meteors or
burning owls across
the profound blank sky of Your face.

12 midnight

My throat is taut against the rope
choking off words and air;
I'm reduced to knotted muscle.
Blood bulges in my skull,
my clenched teeth hold it in;
I bite down on despair.

Death sits on my shoulder like a crow
waiting for my squeezed beet
of a heart to burst
so he can eat my eyes

or like a judge
muttering about sluts and punishment
and licking his lips

or like a dark angel
insidious in his glossy feathers
whispering to me to be easy
on myself. To breathe out finally.
Trust me, he says, caressing
me. *Why suffer?*

A temptation, to sink down
into these definitions.
To become a martyr in reverse,
or food, or trash.

To give up my own words for myself,
my own refusals.
To give up knowing.
To give up pain.
To let go.

2 a.m.

Out of my mouth is coming, at some
distance from me, a thin gnawing sound
which you could confuse with prayer except that
praying is not constrained.

Or is it, Lord?
Maybe it's more like being strangled
than I once thought. Maybe it's
a gasp for air, prayer.
Did those men at Pentecost
want flames to shoot out of their heads?
Did they ask to be tossed
on the ground, gabbling like holy poultry,
eyeballs bulging?

As mine are, as mine are.
There is only one prayer; it is not
the knees in the clean nightgown
on the hooked rug,
I want this, I want that.
Oh far beyond.
Call it *Please.* Call it *Mercy.*
Call it *Not yet, not yet,*
as Heaven threatens to explode
inwards in fire and shredded flesh, and the angels caw.

3 *a.m.*

wind seethes in the leaves around
me the trees exude night

birds night birds yell inside
my ears like stabbed hearts my heart
stutters in my fluttering cloth
body I dangle with strength
going out of me the wind seethes
in my body tattering
the words I clench
my fists hold No
talisman or silver disc my lungs
flail as if drowning I call
on you as witness I did
no crime I was born I have borne I
bear I will be born this is
a crime I will not
acknowledge leaves and wind
hold on to me
I will not give in

6 a.m.

Sun comes up, huge and blaring,
no longer a simile for God.
Wrong address. I've been out there.

Time is relative, let me tell you
I have lived a millennium.

I would like to say my hair turned white
overnight, but it didn't.
Instead it was my heart:
bleached out like meat in water.

Also, I'm about three inches taller.
This is what happens when you drift in space
listening to the gospel
of the red-hot stars.
Pinpoints of infinity riddle my brain,
a revelation of deafness.

At the end of my rope
I testify to silence.
Don't say I'm not grateful.

Most will have only one death.
I will have two.

8 a.m.

When they came to harvest my corpse
(open your mouth, close your eyes)
cut my body from the rope,

surprise, surprise:
I was still alive.

Tough luck, folks,
I know the law:
you can't execute me twice
for the same thing. How nice.

I fell to the clover, breathed it in,
and bared my teeth at them
in a filthy grin.
You can imagine how that went over.

Now I only need to look
out at them through my sky-blue eyes.
They see their own ill will
staring them in the forehead
and turn tail.

Before, I was not a witch.
But now I am one.

Later

My body of skin waxes and wanes
around my true body,

a tender nimbus.
I skitter over the paths and fields
mumbling to myself like crazy,
mouth full of juicy adjectives
and purple berries.
The townsfolk dive headfirst into the bushes
to get out of my way.

My first death orbits my head,
an ambiguous nimbus,
medallion of my ordeal.
No one crosses that circle.

Having been hanged for something
I never said,
I can now say anything I can say.

Holiness gleams on my dirty fingers,
I eat flowers and dung,
two forms of the same thing, I eat mice
and give thanks, blasphemies
gleam and burst in my wake
like lovely bubbles.
I speak in tongues,
my audience is owls.

My audience is God,
because who the hell else could understand me?
Who else has been dead twice?

The words boil out of me,
coil after coil of sinuous possibility.
The cosmos unravels from my mouth,
all fullness, all vacancy.

A few inches down and the soil stops
like a bolted door. A hard frost and that's that
for anything left unharvested.

Why should an old woman suck up the space,
the black roots, red juice that should be going
instead into the children?

Of course she practised magic.
When you're that hungry
you need such hooks and talons.

Held her breath at midnight, uncrossed her fingers,
and owls' feathers sprouted all over her
like mould on meat, but faster.

Saw her myself, hunting mice
in the moonlight. Silent
as the shadow of a hand thrown by a candle.

A good disguise, but I knew it was her
next day, by the white feather
caught in her hair.

She burned extremely, thick fat on fire.
Making grey screams. Giving back
to the air what she took when she shrivelled us.

She might have saved herself
with her white owl's voice
but we cut parts off her first

so she couldn't fly.
The fingers, those are the wings.
We watched her smoulder and got drunk after.

Her heart was the ember
we used to relight our stoves.
This is our culture,

no business of yours.
You have soft feet.
You don't know what it's like,
so close to bedrock.

DOWN

i.

They were wrong about the sun.
It does not go down into
the underworld at night.
The sun leaves merely
and the underworld emerges.
It can happen at any moment.

It can happen in the morning,
you in the kitchen going through
your mild routines.
Plate, cup, knife.
All at once there's no blue, no green,
no warning.

ii.

Old thread, old line
of ink twisting out into the clearness
we call space
where are you leading me this time?

72

Past the stove, past the table,
past the daily horizontal
of the floor, past the cellar,
past the believable,
down into the darkness
where you reverse and shine.

iii.

At first you think they are angels,
these albino voices, these voices
like the unpainted eyes of statues,
these mute voices like gloves
with no hands in them,
these moth voices fluttering
and baffled around your ears,
trying to make you hear them.

What do they need?

You make a cut in yourself,
a little opening
for the pain to get in.
You set loose three drops of your blood.

iv.

This is
the kingdom of the unspoken,
the kingdom of the unspeaking:

all those destroyed by war
all those who are starving
all those beaten to death
and buried in pits, those slit apart
for reasons of expediency or money
all those howling
in locked rooms, all sacrificed
children, all murdered brides,
all suicides.

They say:
Speak for us (to whom)
Some say: *Avenge us* (on whom)
Some say: *Take our place.*
Some say: *Witness.*

Others say (and these are women):
Be happy for us.

74

v.

There is the staircase,
there is the sun.
There is the kitchen,
the plate with toast and strawberry jam,
your subterfuge,
your ordinary mirage.

You stand red-handed.
You want to wash yourself
in earth, in rocks and grass

What are you supposed to do
with all this loss?

My father chops with his axe
and the leaves fall off the trees.
It's nineteen forty-three.
He's splitting wood for the winter.
His gun leans behind the door,
beside his goose-greased workboots.
Smoke comes out of the metal chimney.

At night I sleep in a bunk bed.
The waves stroke the lake.
In the mornings it is so cold
we can see our breath
and the ice on the rocky shore.
My mother rakes the ashes
out from under the oven.

This is comfort and safety,
the sound of chopping in the empty forest,
the smell of smoke.
It's nineteen forty-three.
After it rains we have a bonfire.
The children dance around it,
singing about the war

which is happening elsewhere.
What has become of them, those words
that once shone with such
glossy innocence?
I rolled them in my mouth like marbles,
they tasted pure:
smoke, gun, boots, oven.
The fire. The scattered ashes. The winter forest.

I sit in a pink room;
the chest of drawers
has antique man-bored wormholes.
Isn't there enough of the past
without making more?

It's nineteen forty-three.
It's nineteen ninety-four,
I can hear the sound of the chopping.
It's because of the ocean,
it's because of the war
which won't stay under the waves and leaves.
The carpet smells of ashes.

This is the pink hotel
where everything recurs
and nothing is elsewhere.

IV

VI

MAN IN A GLACIER

Now see: they've found a man in a glacier,
two thousand years old, or three,
with everything intact: shoes, teeth, and arrows,
closed eyes, fur hat, the charm he wore to protect him
from death by snow. They think he must have been
a messenger, done in by bad weather,
and still fresh as a mastodon. Then there's

the box of slides in the cellar
my brother found, the kind we used to
tape between glass. As it turns out
the wrong thing for mildew.
Some cleaning, scraping away those little
flowers of crystallizing earth, and then
a wand of light, and here's my father,
alive or else preserved, younger than all
of us now, dark-haired and skinny,
in baggy trousers, woollen legs tucked into
those lace-up boots of our ancestors,
by a lake, feeding a picnic fire
in the clear blue-tinged air of either
a northern summer or else a film
of aging gelatin spread thinly

with fading colours,
the reds pushing towards pink, the greens greying,

but there. There still. This was all we got,
this echo, this freeze-framed
simulacrum or slight imprint,
in answer to our prayers for everlastingness,

the first time we discovered
we could not stop, or live backwards;
when we opened
our eyes, found we were rocked
with neither love nor malice in the ruthless
icy arms of Chemistry and Physics, our
bad godmothers. It was they
who were present at our birth, who laid
the curse on us: *You will not sleep forever.*

He was sitting in a chair at dinner
and a wave washed over him.
Suddenly, whole beaches
were simply gone.
1947. Lake Superior. Last year.

But the cabin, I said, that one,
the one with the owl —
don't you remember?
Nothing was left. No feathers.

We remained to him in fragments.
Why are you so old, he asked me,
all of a sudden?
Where is this forest? Why am I so cold?
Please take me home.

Outside, the neighbour mowed the lawn.
It's all right here, I said.
There are no bears.
There's food. It isn't snowing.

No. We need more wood, he said.
The winter's on its way.
It will be bad.

The daughters have their parties.
Who can cope?
He's left here in a chair
he can't get out of
in all this snow, or possibly
wallpaper. Wheeled somewhere.
He will have to be sly and stubborn
and not let on.

Another man's hand
coming out of a tweed sleeve that isn't
his, curls on his knee. He can move it with the other
hand. Howling would be uncalled for.

Who knows what he knows?
Many things, but where he is
isn't among them. How did it happen,
this cave, this hovel?
It may or may not be noon.

Time is another element
you never think about

until it's gone.
Things like ceilings, or air.

Someone comes to brush
his hair, wheel him to tea-time.
Old women gather around
in pearls and florals. They want to flirt.
An old man is so rare.
He's a hero just by being here.

They giggle. They disappear
behind the hawthorn bushes
in bloom, or possibly sofas.
Now he's been left alone
with the television turned on
to the weather program, the sound down.

The cold blast sweeps across
the waste field of the afternoon.
Rage occurs,
followed by supper:
something he can't taste,
a brownish texture.

The sun goes down. The trees bend,
they straighten up. They bend.

At eight the youngest daughter comes.
She holds his hand.
She says, *Did they feed you?*
He says no.
He says, *Get me out of here.*
He wants so much to say *please*,
but won't.

After a pause, she says —
he hears her say —
I love you like salt.

A VISIT

Gone are the days
when you could walk on water.
When you could walk.

The days are gone.
Only one day remains,
the one you're in.

The memory is no friend.
It can only tell you
what you no longer have:

a left hand you can use,
two feet that walk.
All the brain's gadgets.

Hello, hello.
The one hand that still works
grips, won't let go.

That is not a train.
There is no cricket.
Let's not panic.

Let's talk about axes,
which kinds are good,
the many names of wood.

This is how to build
a house, a boat, a tent.
No use; the toolbox

refuses to reveal its verbs;
the rasp, the plane, the awl
revert to sullen metal.

Do you recognize anything? I said.
Anything familiar?
Yes, you said. The bed.

Better to watch the stream
that flows across the floor
and is made of sunlight,

the forest made of shadows;
better to watch the fireplace
which is now a beach.

DANCING

It was my father taught my mother
how to dance.
I never knew that.
I thought it was the other way.
Ballroom was their style,
a graceful twirling,
curved arms and fancy footwork,
a green-eyed radio.

There is always more than you know.
There are always boxes
put away in the cellar,
worn shoes and cherished pictures,
notes you find later,
sheet music you can't play.

A woman came on Wednesdays
with tapes of waltzes.
She tried to make him shuffle
around the floor with her.
She said it would be good for him.
He didn't want to.

All those times I was bored
out of my mind. Holding the log
while he sawed it. Holding
the string while he measured, boards,
distances between things, or pounded
stakes into the ground for rows and rows
of lettuces and beets, which I then (bored)
weeded. Or sat in the back
of the car, or sat still in boats,
sat, sat, while at the prow, stern, wheel
he drove, steered, paddled. It
wasn't even boredom, it was looking,
looking hard and up close at the small
details. Myopia. The worn gunwales,
the intricate twill of the seat
cover. The acid crumbs of loam, the granular
pink rock, its igneous veins, the sea-fans
of dry moss, the blackish and then the greying
bristles on the back of his neck.
Sometimes he would whistle, sometimes
I would. The boring rhythm of doing
things over and over, carrying
the wood, drying

the dishes. Such minutiae. It's what
the animals spend most of their time at,
ferrying the sand, grain by grain, from their tunnels,
shuffling the leaves in their burrows. He pointed
such things out, and I would look
at the whorled texture of his square finger, earth under
the nail. Why do I remember it as sunnier
all the time then, although it more often
rained, and more birdsong?
I could hardly wait to get
the hell out of there to
anywhere else. Perhaps though
boredom is happier. It is for dogs or
groundhogs. Now I wouldn't be bored.
Now I would know too much.
Now I would know.

FLOWERS

Right now I am the flower girl.
I bring fresh flowers,
dump out the old ones, the greenish water
that smells like dirty teeth
into the bathroom sink, snip off the stem ends
with surgical scissors I borrowed
from the nursing station,
put them into a jar
I brought from home, because they don't have vases
in this hotel for the ill,
place them on the table beside my father
where he can't see them
because he won't open his eyes.

He lies flattened under the white sheet.
He says he is on a ship,
and I can see it —
the functional white walls, the minimal windows,
the little bells, the rubbery footsteps of strangers,
the whispering all around
of the air-conditioner, or else the ocean,

and he is on a ship;
he's giving us up, giving up everything
but the breath going in
and out of his diminished body;
minute by minute he's sailing slowly away,
away from us and our waving hands
that do not wave.

The women come in, two of them, in blue;
it's no use being kind, in here,
if you don't have hands like theirs —
large and capable, the hands
of plump muscular angels,
the ones that blow trumpets and lift swords.
They shift him carefully, tuck in the corners.
It hurts, but as little as possible.
Pain is their lore. The rest of us
are helpless amateurs.

A suffering you can neither cure nor enter —
there are worse things, but not many.
After a while it makes us impatient.
Can't we do anything but feel sorry?

I sit there, watching the flowers
in their pickle jar. He is asleep, or not.

I think: He looks like a turtle.
Or: He looks erased.
But somewhere in there, at the far end of the tunnel
of pain and forgetting he's trapped in
is the same father I knew before,
the one who carried the green canoe
over the portage, the painter trailing,
myself with the fishing rods, slipping
on the wet boulders and slapping flies.
That was the last time we went there.

There will be a last time for this also,
bringing cut flowers to this white room.
Sooner or later I too
will have to give everything up,
even the sorrow that comes with these flowers,
even the anger,
even the memory of how I brought them
from a garden I will no longer have by then,
and put them beside my dying father,
hoping I could still save him.

TWO DREAMS

In the seven days before his death
I dreamed my father twice.
First by the shore,
the beach, the rocks, the driftwood stumps,
my mother in a blue bathrobe, frantic:
He went into the lake, in all his clothes,
just waded out and sank.
Why did he do that?

I dove to find him —
the shells of crayfish, clam tracks on sand,
drowned stones with their bloom of algae —
but he was too far down.
He still had his hat on.

The second time it was autumn,
we were up on the hill, all the leaves fallen,
by the small cabin that burned down,
each window zinced with frost,
each log restored,
not blurred or faded by dream,
but exact, the way they were.

Such dreams are relentless.

My father is standing there
with his back turned to us
in his winter parka, the hood up.
He never had one like that.

Now he's walking away.
The bright leaves rustle, we can't call,
he doesn't look.

THE TIME

You'd better come down, my brother said.
It's the time. I know death when I see it.
There's a clear look.

The sweet, dire smell of hospitals,
stale piss and disinfectant,
and baby powder.

The nurse said, Has anyone
been away? I said, Me.
Ah, she said. They wait. It's often like that.

My sister said, I was holding
his hand. He winced
like pulling off a bandage,

he frowned. My mother said,
I need some time
with him. Not very long. Alone.

Sitting at noon over the carrot salad
my sister and I compare dreams.

She says, Father was there
in some kind of very strange nightgown
covered with bristles, like a hair shirt.
He was blind, he was stumbling around
bumping into things, and I couldn't stop crying.

I say, Mine was close.
He was still alive, and all of it
was a mistake, but it was our fault.
He couldn't talk, but it was clear
he wanted everything back, the shoes, the binoculars
we'd given away or thrown out.
He was wearing stripes, like a prisoner.
We were trying to be cheerful,
but I wasn't happy to see him:
now we would have to do the whole thing over again.

Who sends us these messages,
oblique and muffled?
What good can they do?

In the daylight we know
what's gone is gone,
but at night it's different.
Nothing gets finished,
not dying, not mourning;
the dead repeat themselves, like clumsy drunks
lurching sideways through the doors
we open to them in sleep;
these slurred guests, never entirely welcome,
even those we have loved the most,
especially those we have loved the most,
returning from where we shoved them
away too quickly:
from under the ground, from under the water,
they clutch at us, they clutch at us,
we won't let go.

It's Christmas, and the green wreaths,
festive and prickly, with their bright red
holly berries, dot the graves,

the shocked mouths grief has made
and keeps on making:
round silent Ohs,
leafy and still alive
that hurt when you touch them.

Look, they are everywhere: Oh. Oh. Oh. Oh.
What else can be said?

Strange how we decorate pain.
These ribbons, for instance,
and the small hard teardrops of blood.
Who are they for?
Do we think the dead care?

It's so cold today
even the birds, those flurries
of light and fever,
freeze in the air.

The bare trees crack overhead
as we place our flowers
already stiff with ice.

In the spring the flowers will melt,
also the berries,
and something will come to eat them.
We will go around
in these circles for a time,
winter summer winter,
and, after more time, not.

This is a good thought.

In the full moon you dream more.
I know where I am: the Ottawa River
far up, where the dam goes across.
Once, midstorm, in the wide cold water
upstream, two long canoes full
of children tipped, and they all held hands
and sang till the chill reached their hearts.
I suppose in our waking lives that's the best
we can hope for, if you think of that moment
stretched out for years.
                         Once, my father
and I paddled seven miles
along a lake near here
at night, with the trees like a pelt of dark
hackles, and the waves hardly moving.
In the moonlight the way ahead was clear
and obscure both. I was twenty
and impatient to get there, thinking
such a thing existed.
                 None of this
is in the dream, of course. Just the thick square-
edged shape of the dam, and eastward
the hills of sawdust from the mill, gleaming as white

as dunes. To the left, stillness; to the right,
the swirling foam of rapids
over sharp rocks and snags; and below that, my father,
moving away downstream
in his boat, so skilfully
although dead, I remember now; but no longer as old.
He wears his grey hat, and evidently
he can see again. There now,
he's around the corner. He's heading eventually
to the sea. Not the real one, with its sick whales
and oil slicks, but the other sea, where there can still be
safe arrivals.

    Only a dream, I think, waking
to the sound of nothing.
Not nothing. I heard: it was a beach, or shore,
and someone far off, walking.
Nowhere familiar. Somewhere I've been before.
It always takes a long time
to decipher where you are.

V

VERMILION FLYCATCHER,
SAN PEDRO RIVER, ARIZONA

The river's been here, violent, right where we're standing,
you can tell by the trash caught overhead in the trees.
Now it's a trickle, and we're up to our knees
in late-spring yellowing weeds. A vermilion
flycatcher darts down, flutters up, perches.
Stick a pin in your thumb, the bead of blood
would be his colour. He's filled with joy
and the tranced rage of sex. How he conjures,
with his cry like a needle. A punctuation. A bone button

on fire. Everything bad you can imagine
is happening somewhere else, or happened
here, a hundred years or centuries
ago. He sings, and there's the murder:
you see it, forming under
the shimmering air, a man with brown
or white skin lying reversed
in the vanished water, a spear
or bullet in his back. At the ford, where the deer
come at dusk to cross and drink
and be ambushed. The red bird

is sitting on the same tree, intensely
bright in the sun that gleams on cruelty, on broken
skullbone, arrow, spur. Vultures cluster,
he doesn't care. He and his other-coloured mate
ignore everything but their own rapture.
Who knows what they remember?
Birds never dream, being their own.
Dreams, I mean. As for you, the river
that isn't there is the same one
you could drown in, face down.

THE MOMENT

The moment when, after many years
of hard work and a long voyage
you stand in the centre of your room,
house, half-acre, square mile, island, country,
knowing at last how you got there,
and say, *I own this,*

is the same moment the trees unloose
their soft arms from around you,
the birds take back their language,
the cliffs fissure and collapse,
the air moves back from you like a wave
and you can't breathe.

No, they whisper. *You own nothing.*
You were a visitor, time after time
climbing the hill, planting the flag, proclaiming.
We never belonged to you.
You never found us.
It was always the other way round.

You wake up filled with dread.
There seems no reason for it.
Morning light sifts through the window,
there is birdsong,
you can't get out of bed.

It's something about the crumpled sheets
hanging over the edge like jungle
foliage, the terry slippers gaping
their dark pink mouths for your feet,
the unseen breakfast — some of it
in the refrigerator you do not dare
to open — you will not dare to eat.

What prevents you? The future. The future tense,
immense as outer space.
You could get lost there.
No. Nothing so simple. The past, its density
and drowned events pressing you down,
like sea water, like gelatin
filling your lungs instead of air.

Forget all that and let's get up.
Try moving your arm.
Try moving your head.
Pretend the house is on fire
and you must run or burn.
No, that one's useless.
It's never worked before.

Where is it coming from, this echo,
this huge No that surrounds you,
silent as the folds of the yellow
curtains, mute as the cheerful

Mexican bowl with its cargo
of mummified flowers?
(You chose the colours of the sun,
not the dried neutrals of shadow.
God knows you've tried.)

Now here's a good one:
you're lying on your deathbed.
You have one hour to live.
Who is it, exactly, you have needed
all these years to forgive?

Walking through the ruins
on your way to work
that do not look like ruins
with the sunlight pouring over
the seen world
like hail or melted
silver, that bright
and magnificent, each leaf
and stone quickened and specific in it,
and you can't hold it,
you can't hold any of it. Distance surrounds you,
marked out by the ends of your arms
when they are stretched to their fullest.
You can go no farther than this,
you think, walking forward,
pushing the distance in front of you
like a metal cart on wheels
with its barriers and horizontals.
Appearance melts away from you,
the offices and pyramids
on the horizon shimmer and cease.
No one can enter that circle
you have made, that clean circle

of dead space you have made
and stay inside,
mourning because it is clean.

Then there's the girl, in the white dress,
meaning purity, or the failure
to be any colour. She has no hands, it's true.
The scream that happened to the air
when they were taken off
surrounds her now like an aureole
of hot sand, of no sound.
Everything has bled out of her.

Only a girl like this
can know what's happened to you.
If she were here she would
reach out her arms towards
you now, and touch you
with her absent hands
and you would feel nothing, but you would be
touched all the same.

THE SIGNER

In city after city
in an area of darkness behind my head
stands a woman dressed in black,
even the stockings: my unknown twin.

Only her hands are moving:
they catch the light and throw it
into the silence,
which for some here is total.

In her hands, deft as a knitter's
but quicker, my words turn solid,
become a gesture, a skein,
a semaphore of the body
for those who listen with their eyes.

Unable to see her, I speak
in a kind of blindness, not knowing
what dance is being made of me,

what puns of the thumb, tough
similes of the fingers,
how I translate into bone.

(Yet it is not a translation
you build here, mute sister,
left-handed shadow cast by an absence
that moves you nevertheless to love:

together we are practising
for the place where all the languages
will be finalized and
one; and the hands also.)

A FIRE PLACE

Here is the place where the lightning fire one time
almost got us. Where the heroic youngish
(now dead) men in their chequered flannel
shirts with the sleeves rolled up and their high-laced
lumberjacks' (obsolete) boots once fought it
with hand-pumps and axes to a damp and acrid
standstill. Where the charred trunks lay smouldering.
The whole thing a gash (they said) in the forest. A scar.
Where then poplar seeped in and over, feeding on ashes,
    and (purple)
fireweed, and (blue) berries, and the bears, and us
with our lard pails and tin cups, our jelly
sandwiches at lunchtime, skinning our knees on the sooty
rocks, smudging our hands
and mouths with black and blue, in our summer clothing (since
torn into dustcloths, thrown out and rotted away).
Now that bright random clearing
or burn, or meadow if you like, is gone
also, and there's scrubland, a light-green
sticky new forest. Earth does such things
to itself: furrowing, cracking apart, bursting
into flame. It rips openings in itself, which it struggles
(or not) to skin over. The moon

doesn't care about its own
craters and bruises. Only we can regret
the perishing of the burned place.
Only we could call it a wound.

STATUARY

Wingtips, fingertips, nipples, and penises —
the parts we once flew with are broken
away first by whoever it is with a hammer,
to whom the body's flights are an affront.
Who are you, you who shamble and roll
like an unseen boulder or troll through parks and cemeteries
and wish to keep us earthbound?
After that the noses go, and then
the toes, if any. You want to keep us from walking,
however heavily, on our limestone feet
in search of our lost trajectories.
Then our arms. Enfolding is taken from us,
and clasp. Our mouths erode in the rain
you send, and all our bright definite
nouns and quick verbs with them.
We are ground down to our torsos,
just those, and our heads, increasingly
blunted and smoothed of gesture,
each of us a vestigial stump
topped with a doorknob. Then
headless, a stub, like a whale's tooth or a tongue
cut out of a face and frozen.

Even this isn't enough for you.
You won't be content until we're toppled,
like you, by frost-heave or vandals, and lie melting
in the uncut grass, like you. In the tall weeds. In the
      young trees.
Until we're rubble. Like you. Until we're pebbles
on the shore of a vast lake that doesn't (like you)
      exist yet.
Until we're liquid, like you; like the small whirlpools
an oar makes drawn slowly through water,
those darkly shining swirls the shape of a galaxy,
those knotholes the world turns itself
      inside out through
for us, for a moment, the nothingness
that by its moving
edges defines time. That lets us see down
and into. That lets us fly
and embody, like you. Until we are like you.

I.

Through the slit of our open window, the wind
comes in and flows around us, nothingness
in motion, like time. The power of what is not there.
The snow empties itself down, a shadow turning
to indigo, obliterating
everything out there, roofs, cars, garbage cans,
dead flowerstalks, dog turds, it doesn't matter.
You could read this as indifference
on the part of the universe, or else a relentless
forgiveness: all of our
scratches and blots and mortal
wounds and patched-up jobs
wiped clean in the snow's huge erasure.

I feel it as a pressure,
an added layer:
above, the white waterfall of snow
thundering down; then attic, moth-balled
sweaters, nomadic tents,
the dried words of old letters;

then stairs, then children, cats and radiators, peeling
    paint,
us in our bed, the afterglow
of a smoky fire, our one candle flickering;
below us, the kitchen in the dark, the wink
of pots on shelves; then books and tools, then cellar
and furnace, greying dolls, a bicycle,
the whole precarious geology of house
crisscrossed with hidden mousetrails,
and under that a buried river
that seeps up through the cement
floor every spring,
and the tree roots snouting their slow way
into the drains;
under that, the bones
of our ancestors, or if not theirs, someone's,
mixed with a biomass of nematodes;
under that, bedrock, then molten
stone and the earth's fiery core;
and sideways, out into the city, street
and corner store and mall
and underpass, then barns and ruined woodlands,
    continent
and island, oceans, mists
of story drifting
on the tide like seaweed, animal

species crushed and blinking out,
and births and illnesses, hatred and love infra-
red, compassion fleshtone, prayer ultra-
violet; then rumours, alternate waves
of sad peace and sad war,
and then the air, and then the scintillating ions,
and then the stars. That's where
we are.

2.

Some centuries ago, when we lived at the edge
of the forest, on nights like this
you would have put on your pelt of a bear
and shambled off to prowl and hulk
among the trees, and be a silhouette of human
fears against the snowbank.
I would have chosen fox;
I liked the jokes,
the doubling back on my tracks,
and, let's face it, the theft.
Back then, I had many forms:
the sliding in and out
of my own slippery eelskin,
and yours as well; we were each other's

iridescent glove, the deft body
all sleight-of-hand and illusion.
Once we were lithe as pythons, quick
and silvery as herring, and we still are, momentarily,
except our knees hurt.
Right now we're content to huddle
under the shed feathers of duck and goose
as the wind pours like a river
we swim in by keeping still,
like trout in a current.
                              Every cell
in our bodies has renewed itself
so many times since then, there's
not much left, my love,
of the originals. We're footprints
becoming limestone, or think of it
as coal becoming diamond. Less
flexible, but more condensed;
and no more scales or aliases,
at least on the outside. Though we've accumulated,
despite ourselves, other disguises:
you as a rumpled elephant-
hide suitcase with white fur,
me as a bramble bush. Well, the hair
was always difficult. Then there's
the eye problems: too close, too far, you're a blur.

I used to say I'd know you anywhere,
but it's getting harder.

3.

This is the solstice, the still point
of the sun, its cusp and midnight,
the year's threshold
and unlocking, where the past
lets go of and becomes the future;
the place of caught breath, the door
of a vanished house left ajar.

Taking hands like children
lost in a six-dimensional
forest, we step across.
The walls of the house fold themselves down,
and the house turns
itself inside out, as a tulip does
in its last full-blown moment, and our candle
flares up and goes out, and the only common
sense that remains to us is touch,

as it will be, later, some other
century, when we will seem to each other
even less what we were.

But the trick is just to hold on
through all appearances; and so we do,
and yes, I know it's you;
and that is what we will come to, sooner
or later, when it's even darker
than it is now, when the snow is colder,
when it's darkest and coldest
and candles are no longer any use to us
and the visibility is zero: *Yes.*
It's still you. It's still you.

In the burned house I am eating breakfast.
You understand: there is no house, there is no breakfast,
yet here I am.

The spoon which was melted scrapes against
the bowl which was melted also.
No one else is around.

Where have they gone to, brother and sister,
mother and father? Off along the shore,
perhaps. Their clothes are still on the hangers,

their dishes piled beside the sink,
which is beside the woodstove
with its grate and sooty kettle,

every detail clear,
tin cup and rippled mirror.
The day is bright and songless,

the lake is blue, the forest watchful.
In the east a bank of cloud
rises up silently like dark bread.

126

I can see the swirls in the oilcloth,
I can see the flaws in the glass,
those flares where the sun hits them.

I can't see my own arms and legs
or know if this is a trap or blessing,
finding myself back here, where everything

in this house has long been over,
kettle and mirror, spoon and bowl,
including my own body,

including the body I had then,
including the body I have now
as I sit at this morning table, alone and happy,

bare child's feet on the scorched floorboards
(I can almost see)
in my burning clothes, the thin green shorts

and grubby yellow T-shirt
holding my cindery, non-existent,
radiant flesh. Incandescent.